Note To Self

Affirmations to Young Queens

Author: Celina Monique McMillian, MSW

Illustrator: Autumn N. Hayes

Published by Melanin Origins LLC
PO Box 122123; Arlington, TX 76012

First Edition

Library of Congress Control Number: 2017914407

ISBN: 978-1-62676-844-4 hardback
ISBN: 978-1-62676-842-0 paperback
ISBN: 978-1-62676-843-7 ebook

Dedication

This book is dedicated to my mother Janice, my Goddaughter Ilah and to ALL Queens EVERYWHERE! Continue leaving your magic everywhere you go!

Mother, I love you and thank you for ALWAYS being my ROQ! You have molded me into greatness and I do not know what I would be without you. Because of who you are, I am, and it doesn't get any better than that.

Ilah, you are an amazing kid and the light of my life. You make me laugh and you teach me to enjoy the "small things". It is an honor to be your Godmother. I will ALWAYS be by your side to cheer you on or simply "Ju Ju on the Beat."

From Legendary Queens, like Monica, Michelle Obama, Tiffany Haddish and Issa Rae, to my family, friends, mentors and women who I have encountered along the way, THANK YOU!! Your kind words, posts of wisdom, and just being yourselves keep me going when things get difficult. Someone once asked me, "Who motivates the motivator?" Due to your support, both intentional and unintentional, I am able to accomplish great things like writing this book.

An affirmation is something that you tell yourself, for encouragement, but you have to believe it's true. At times we have to remind ourselves verbally to see it through.

1

Read this book daily to motivate and inspire you. View it as a "Note to Self" and know that greatness lies within you.

I am beautifully, fearfully, and wonderfully made!
That's our baby girl!
MY BLACK IS BEAUTIFUL

I am
talented
and unique!

15

I am
greatness!

I love myself!

17

I will make good choices!

The things that make me different, also make me who I am!

Friend

CPSIA information can be obtained at www.ICGtesting.com
Printed in the USA
BVIW12n0250170118
505473BV00001B/1